GEORGE WASHINGTON AND ALEXANDER HAMILTON

By Katie Kawa

Gareth Stevens
PUBLISHING

Please visit our website, www.garethstevens.com. For a free color catalog of all our high-quality books, call toll free 1-800-542-2595 or fax 1-877-542-2596.

Library of Congress Cataloging-in-Publication Data

Names: Kawa, Katie, author.
Title: George Washington and Alexander Hamilton / Katie Kawa.
Description: New York : Gareth Stevens Publishing, [2022] | Series: History's famous friendships | Includes bibliographical references and index.
Identifiers: LCCN 2020034442 (print) | LCCN 2020034443 (ebook) | ISBN 9781538264911 (library binding) | ISBN 9781538264898 (paperback) | ISBN 9781538264904 (set) | ISBN 9781538264928 (ebook)
Subjects: LCSH: Washington, George, 1732-1799--Friends and associates--Juvenile literature. | Hamilton, Alexander, 1757-1804--Friends and associates--Juvenile literature. | Statesmen--United States--Biography--Juvenile literature. | Founding Fathers of the United States--Biography--Juvenile literature. | United States--History--Revolution, 1775-1783--Juvenile literature. | United States--History--1783-1815--Juvenile literature.
Classification: LCC E302.5 .K39 2022 (print) | LCC E302.5 (ebook) | DDC 973.3092/2 [B]--dc23
LC record available at https://lccn.loc.gov/2020034442
LC ebook record available at https://lccn.loc.gov/2020034443

First Edition

Published in 2022 by
Gareth Stevens Publishing
111 East 14th Street, Suite 349
New York, NY 10003

Designer: Katelyn E. Reynolds
Editor: Therese Shea

Photo credits: Cvr, pp. 1 (Hamilton) Gift of Henry G. Marquand, 1881 /The Metropolitan Museum of Art; cvr, p. 1 (Washington) Rogers Fund, 1907/The Metropolitan Museum of Art; cvr, pp. 1-32 (background) wawritto/Shutterstock.com; pp. 1-32 (frame) Olesia Misty/Shutterstock.com; cvr, pp. 1-32 (border) Vasya Kobelev/Shutterstock.com; p. 5 Universal History Archive/Getty Images; pp. 7, 14, 16, 17 courtesy of the Library of Congress; p. 9 Buyenlarge/Getty Images; p. 9 (map) negoworks/iStock/Getty Images Plus; pp. 11, 13 (Tench Tilghman, Henry Knox) Hulton Archive/Getty Images; pp. 12, 13 (John Laurens, Nathanael Greene, Alexander Hamilton), 23 Smith Collection/Gado/Getty Images; p. 13 (Marquis de Lafayette) Grafissimo/DigitalVision Vectors/Getty Images; p. 15 Gift of John Stewart Kennedy, 1897/The Metropolitan Museum of Art; p. 19 (cabinet) PhotoQuest/Getty Images; pp. 19, 21 courtesy of the Architect of the Capitol; p. 22 courtesy of the New York Public Library; p. 24 Stock Montage/Getty Images; p. 25 National Portrait Gallery, Smithsonian Institution; acquired as a gift to the nation through the generosity of the Donald W. Reynolds Foundation; p. 27 (monument) traveler1116/E+/Getty Images; p. 27 Bettmann/Getty Images; p. 28 Walter McBride/WireImage/Getty Images; p. 29 Ed Vebell/Getty Images.

Printed in the United States of America

CPSIA compliance information: Batch #CSGS22: For further information contact Gareth Stevens, New York, New York at 1-800-542-2595.

Find us on

CONTENTS

Words in the Glossary appear in **bold** type the first time they are used in the text.

FRIENDS AND FOUNDING FATHERS

The Founding Fathers were a group of men who helped build what's now the United States of America. They fought for freedom from Great Britain during a war called the American Revolution. They also set up a **democratic** form of government called a republic for the new country. In this government, citizens elect officials to make laws and a president to make sure the laws are followed.

George Washington and Alexander Hamilton were two important Founding Fathers. They worked together to help create the new nation and formed a friendship along the way.

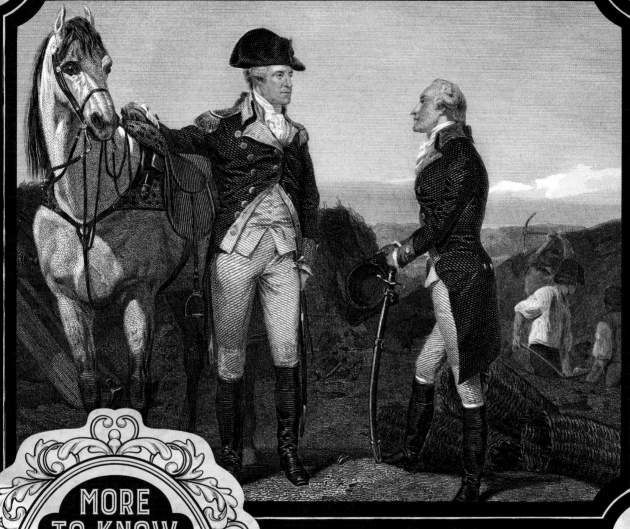

George Washington (left) became the first president of the United States. Alexander Hamilton (right) was one of the people Washington trusted to help him run the country.

WASHINGTON BEFORE THE WAR

Alexander Hamilton and other young **revolutionaries** looked up to George Washington. Washington was born in February 1732 in the British colony of Virginia. His family owned a lot of land. By 1752, Washington was in charge of a large home and farm known as Mount Vernon.

Washington became a military leader during the French and Indian War, which lasted from 1754 to 1763. During this war, the British and their Native American **allies** fought the French and their Native American allies.

MORE TO KNOW

GEORGE WASHINGTON IS BEST KNOWN FOR FIGHTING AGAINST THE BRITISH DURING THE AMERICAN REVOLUTION. HOWEVER, DURING THE FRENCH AND INDIAN WAR, HE FOUGHT FOR THE BRITISH.

Washington is shown here on a white horse during the French and Indian War. During this war, two of his horses were shot while he was riding them.

A VERY DIFFERENT STORY

Alexander Hamilton's early life was very different from Washington's. His exact birth year isn't known. It's believed he was born in either 1755 or 1757. He was born on the island of Nevis in the Caribbean Sea. When Alexander was young, his father left the family. His mother died shortly after.

Hamilton had a hard life, but he was a great writer. People in his community raised money to send him to school in the American colonies. By 1773, he had settled in New York City.

MORE TO KNOW

WHEN HAMILTON WAS A TEENAGER, A **HURRICANE** HIT THE ISLAND OF ST. CROIX, WHERE HE WAS WORKING. HE WROTE A LETTER ABOUT THE STORM. THAT LETTER **INSPIRED** PEOPLE TO SEND HIM TO AMERICA.

8

U.S.

Nevis

St. Croix

Hamilton was much younger than Washington.
He grew up without land or close family.
However, he wanted to make a name for himself
in America. Washington would later help him.

9

JOINING THE REVOLUTION

Hamilton and Washington came from different backgrounds. However, they shared a belief in American independence, or freedom, from Britain. In 1775, Washington was named the leader of the Continental army, which was the American army in the American Revolution. Hamilton joined in the fighting too.

In January 1777, Hamilton's soldiers helped Washington's troops during the Battle of Princeton in New Jersey. The Continental army won the battle. Washington noticed Hamilton's bravery. He asked Hamilton to join his **staff**. Hamilton agreed.

MORE TO KNOW

IN 1769, HAMILTON WROTE A LETTER TO A FRIEND. IN IT, HE SAID, "I WISH THERE WAS A WAR." HE BELIEVED FIGHTING IN A WAR WOULD HELP HIM MAKE A NAME FOR HIMSELF AND RISE IN THE WORLD.

Another military leader wanted Hamilton (above) to work for him. However, Hamilton accepted Washington's offer.

PART OF THE "FAMILY"

In 1777, Hamilton officially joined Washington's staff as an aide-de-camp. That's a French term for "camp assistant," or a person who helps a military leader. Washington had many aides-de-camp, but Hamilton stood out. He was smart, wrote well, and spoke French. This was useful because the French were helping the Americans during the war.

Hamilton often wrote to other leaders for Washington and delivered important messages for him. He became part of what was known as Washington's military "family."

George Washington

Washington's "Family"

John Laurens
- wanted the abolition, or end, of slavery
- killed in battle in 1782

Marquis de Lafayette
- birth name was Gilbert du Motier
- joined Washington in 1777 and became like a son to him

Tench Tilghman
- asked to serve under Washington in 1776
- was Washington's longest-serving aide

Henry Knox
- a leader in the Continental army
- Washington's close friend who became U.S. secretary of war

Nathanael Greene
- served under Washington in major battles
- one of the most trusted members of Washington's "family"

Alexander Hamilton
- was asked to join Washington after his battlefield efforts
- became a friend and later the U.S. secretary of the treasury

Hamilton was one of the most important members of Washington's military family. These are some others who became the future president's close aides, advisers, and friends.

WALKING AWAY

Hamilton and Washington worked well together, but Hamilton wanted more. He believed that Washington was holding him back. Hamilton wanted to take a more active part in the war. He thought that would help him become successful in the future. However, Washington didn't send him into battle.

In 1781, Hamilton's anger turned into action. He resigned, or left his job. After he left, Hamilton wrote about Washington in a letter. He said, "For three years past, I have felt no friendship for him."

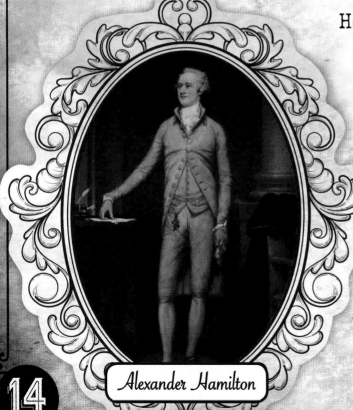

Alexander Hamilton

Washington Crossing the Delaware

Washington earned glory and respect in battle, as the famous painting above shows. Hamilton wanted to do the same. This led to a fight between them.

THE BATTLE OF YORKTOWN

Alexander Hamilton didn't stay away from the action for long. Later in 1781, George Washington finally offered him a position in the field. That meant Hamilton could lead troops into battle. In October 1781, Hamilton and his soldiers helped the Continental army win the Battle of Yorktown in Virginia.

The Battle of Yorktown was the last major battle fought in the American Revolution. In 1783, the war with Great Britain ended. The United States was free of British rule.

Alexander Hamilton

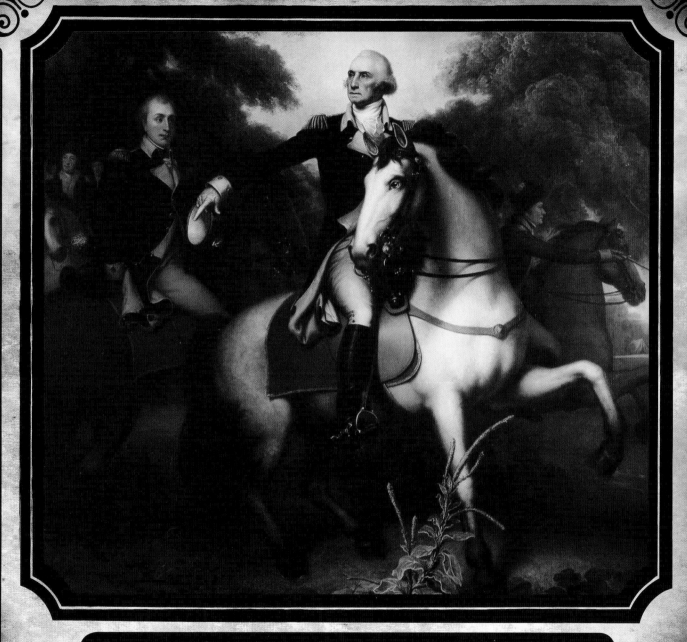

Shown here is a famous painting of Washington before the Battle of Yorktown.
Hamilton can be seen riding his horse on the right.

CHOOSING THE CABINET

Washington was a hero after the war. The American people trusted him. In 1789, he was elected the first president of the United States. He then set up a cabinet. This was a group of people who would give him advice and help him run the country.

Washington knew Hamilton was smart. Hamilton had earned his trust during the war too. He named Hamilton secretary of the treasury. This meant Hamilton was in charge of all matters dealing with money in the new country.

MORE TO KNOW

AFTER THE AMERICAN REVOLUTION, HAMILTON LIVED IN NEW YORK. ONCE WASHINGTON BECAME PRESIDENT, HE MOVED FROM VIRGINIA TO NEW YORK. THAT WAS THE U.S. CAPITAL UNTIL 1790, WHEN PHILADELPHIA BECAME THE CAPITAL.

Alexander Hamilton

George Washington

Henry Knox

Thomas Jefferson

Edmund Randolph

Washington's cabinet

In 1787, Hamilton and Washington went to the meetings in Philadelphia, Pennsylvania, that became known as the Constitutional Convention. There, the Founding Fathers planned and wrote the U.S. Constitution, which set up the country's **federal** government.

WASHINGTON ON HIS SIDE

During the American Revolution, Washington and Hamilton worked well together. However, their friendship seemed even stronger during Washington's time as president. Washington agreed with Hamilton on many important things, including the creation of a national bank.

Some members of the cabinet started to feel left out. As secretary of state, Thomas Jefferson was in charge of dealing with other countries. He often disagreed with Hamilton. He didn't like that Washington seemed to follow Hamilton's advice more than his.

MORE TO KNOW

JEFFERSON AND HAMILTON DISAGREED STRONGLY. IN FACT, THEY HELPED FORM DIFFERENT **POLITICAL PARTIES**. HAMILTON LED THE FEDERALISTS, WHO WANTED A STRONG FEDERAL GOVERNMENT. JEFFERSON LED THE DEMOCRATIC-REPUBLICANS, WHO WANTED STATES TO HAVE MORE POWER.

Washington (right) is shown here with Jefferson (sitting) and Hamilton (standing). The president sometimes found himself in the middle of their disagreements. He often sided with Hamilton.

SAYING GOODBYE

Washington didn't want to be president forever. He knew it was important for the young country to have a new leader. He also wanted to spend time with his family as a regular citizen of the nation he helped create.

In 1796, Washington was ready to tell the country he wasn't running for president again. He turned to Hamilton for help. Hamilton helped him write his farewell address. They worked together to find the best way for Washington to say goodbye.

pages from Washington's farewell address

MORE TO KNOW

HAMILTON LEFT WASHINGTON'S CABINET IN 1795. HOWEVER, THE TWO MEN STAYED FRIENDS. WASHINGTON STILL LOOKED TO HAMILTON FOR HELP AND ADVICE.

Washington's farewell address became one of the most famous speeches in U.S. history.

WORKING
TOGETHER AGAIN

Hamilton's life got harder after he left Washington's cabinet. In 1797, Washington sent him a present to show his **support**. Washington called the gift "a **token** of my . . . friendship." He reminded Hamilton, "I remain your **sincere** friend."

In 1798, Washington was asked to lead an army in case the United States went to war with France. He asked for Hamilton to be his **second-in-command**. Washington believed his friend was the best choice for the job. The war didn't happen, though.

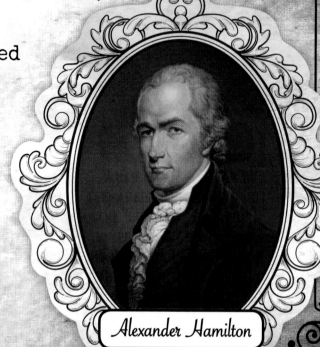

Alexander Hamilton

About making Hamilton his second-in-command, Washington said, "I know not where a more competent [smarter] choice could be made."

THE ENDS OF THEIR STORIES

On December 14, 1799, George Washington died. Hamilton wrote that he owed a lot to "the kindness of the General." He also said that Washington's support had been "essential," or very important, to him.

Hamilton's life was harder without Washington. He supported Thomas Jefferson over Aaron Burr, another Founding Father, in the presidential election of 1800. This made Burr angry, and their fighting continued for several years. On July 11, 1804, Burr shot Hamilton in a duel. Hamilton died the next day.

MORE TO KNOW

HAMILTON'S WIFE ELIZABETH HELPED RAISE MONEY TO BUILD THE WASHINGTON MONUMENT, HONORING THE PRESIDENT, IN WASHINGTON, DC.

Washington monument

A duel was a fight using guns or swords to settle an argument between two people. Witnesses made sure certain rules were followed.

MAKING HISTORY TOGETHER

George Washington and Alexander Hamilton helped make the United States the country it is today. They didn't always agree, and they weren't always close friends. They had fights, and sometimes they trusted other people more. However, they always found their way back to each other.

Today, more and more people want to learn about Hamilton and Washington's friendship because of the *Hamilton* musical. Their friendship shows what people can do when they work together to make their country better!

MORE TO KNOW

IN *HAMILTON*, WASHINGTON CALLS HAMILTON HIS "RIGHT-HAND MAN." THAT'S ANOTHER NAME FOR HIS SECOND-IN-COMMAND, THE PERSON HE TRUSTS THE MOST.

Washington and Hamilton's friendship grew along with the country they created. Together, they made history.

GLOSSARY

ally: one of two or more people or groups who work together

democratic: describing a form of government in which all citizens participate

federal: having to do with the national government

hurricane: a powerful storm that forms over water and causes heavy rainfall and high winds

inspire: to cause someone to want to do something

political party: a group of people with the same ideas for running a government

revolutionary: one who fights in a revolution, which is a war to overthrow a government

second-in-command: one who has the second highest position in a group, right below the leader

sincere: true

staff: a group of people who help a leader

support: the act of giving aid or showing someone you care about them. Also, to agree with or approve of something.

token: a small gift you keep to remind you of something

For More Information

Books

Hally, Ashleigh. *George Washington*. New York, NY: AV2 by Weigl, 2019.

Morlock, Rachael. *The Real Story Behind the Founding Fathers*. New York, NY: PowerKids Press, 2020.

Shea, Therese. *Alexander Hamilton: Founding Father and Treasury Secretary*. New York, NY: Enslow Publishing, 2018.

Websites

Alexander Hamilton
www.brainpop.com/socialstudies/ushistory/alexanderhamilton/
This website features a video, quiz, and other activities about Alexander Hamilton.

American Revolution
www.dkfindout.com/us/history/american-revolution/
Find facts about the American Revolution and the people who played a part in it.

George Washington's Mount Vernon
www.mountvernon.org
Take a trip to Washington's home to learn more about his life and friends, including Hamilton.

INDEX